in Search of Eden

in Search OF Eden

by Frederick Drimmer

Designs by Sally Goodling

Published by The C. R. Gibson Company

Acknowledgments appear on page 56

Library of Congress Catalog Card Number: 73-86687
ISBN: 0-8378-1750-1

Contents

Chapter 1

IN THE BEGINNING

In the beginning God created the heaven and the earth.
And the earth was without form, and void; and darkness was upon the face
of the deep. And the Spirit of God moved upon the face of the waters.

Genesis 1:1, 2

On a clear night we can look up into the immensity of space and see the cheerful twinkling of a great host of stars and the warm, steady glow of the planets. They shine like the lights in a million faraway windows.

Is there life out there? No one knows. We have sent men to the moon and spaceships into the far reaches of the solar system, but we have found no sign that life exists on other planets. Out of millions of heavenly bodies, the earth is the only one known to be inhabited.

The earth whirls on and on through the awesome void. It is like a snug ark on which we are all passengers. We cannot complain, for the Great Designer who made our planet supplied us with the things we need for our voyage. To give us light, energy, and warmth, He set the sun in the sky. To soften its burning rays, He surrounded our planet with an envelope of atmosphere. To hold us safely and securely in place, He established the powerful force of gravity.

The Lord provided water, air, and everything else necessary to life. He provided the green plant, that catches the sunlight from outer space, blends it with water and carbon dioxide, and makes food for us to eat and oxygen to breathe.

Our space ark is a small one, no more than eight thousand miles in diameter. It has room for only a limited number of passengers — and for only a limited quantity of provisions for the journey.

The Laws of Nature

God established rules for the successful operation of Spaceark Earth — the laws of nature. The most basic of these laws is that nothing shall be wasted.

Nature is the original conservationist. She has no junkyards that she fills with the hulks of old automobiles, washing machines, and refrigerators, to lie rusting in the sun. She makes no plastic containers or soda cans to litter the landscape. She throws nothing away. Everything that she creates she uses over and over again.

How else would we have enough to last on our space ark's long voyage?

Only yesterday, it seems, we learned nature's principle of recycling and we began, in a small way, to reprocess newsprint, rubber, metal, and bottles so we could use them again. But Mother Nature has been recycling since the beginning. The moment a tree falls to the ground, she goes to work on it. A host of insects lay their eggs beneath the cracking bark and draw nourishment from the tree. Fungus grows all over it and helps it to decompose. So do hordes of bacteria. Gradually the tree decays and dissolves into its basic elements. It gives these elements back to the soil, enriching it so that more trees can spring up.

The Web of Life

A word we hear more and more today is *ecosystem.* An ecosystem is a combination of living things and their nonliving surroundings.

There are huge ecosystems and small ones. The fallen tree and its community of insects, bacteria, and fungi form a small ecosystem. The tree may, in turn, be part of a larger ecosystem, a forest. A pond, with its water plants, fishes, insects, turtles, and snakes, forms another ecosystem. So does a seashore, a tropical sea, or a prairie. The ecosystems help to make up the life-support system of our space ark.

Each ecosystem contains a many-stranded web of life in which every living thing is interwoven with many other living things and the environment. Each plant or animal depends on those around it and sometimes on others far off.

In the forest the birds depend on the trees for shelter, and in them they build nests to rear their young. The insects find breeding places and food in the trees, and drop fluids rich in calcium to the ground. The birds feed on the insects, and their wastes and those of other animals also fall to the earth. Bacteria in the ground feed on the wastes and convert them into nitrogen and other elements that the trees need. The worms ceaselessly devour the soil and stir it, making it more fertile. Rabbits and field mice nibble the tender shoots of the trees; hawks, owls, and weasels feast on these little animals. Deep in the ground, the roots of the trees, seeking water, pierce down through cracking bedrock and help break it into more soil. So everything in nature acts upon the things around it. We call the study of living things and their relationships *ecology*.

Everything in nature is used, changed, and used again. So it has been for millions of years. The atoms of oxygen that we breathe today were manufactured by plants and were carried to us by the wind. Once, perhaps, they were joined with other atoms in a glass of water that George Washington drank at Mount Vernon. Once they might have been vapor in a cloud drifting over the Mediterranean Sea. Once they could have been part of the water of the river Jordan, in which Jesus was baptized. For every atom has been in faraway places and times, and part of many lives. That is nature's economy.

Although nature wastes nothing, she produces life abundantly, in endlessly varied forms. There is not just one kind of mammal, bird, tree, fish, flower, or insect, but many. Because nature has so many different forms and kinds of life, they hold each other in check. Each has a place, a value, an importance. If one kind were to disappear altogether, who can tell what the effect might be on the things around it?

With all different kinds of wonderful things — trees, plants, animals, water, soil, metals — the Lord stocked our planet. He supplied enough for a paradise on earth. Provided that man used everything with care and thrift. Provided that man did not become so numerous that Spaceark Earth could no longer contain him.

As Charles F. Kettering said: "We should all be concerned with the future because we will have to spend the rest of our lives here."

A Portent and a Warning

Now the population is increasing vastly. The space ark is filling up rapidly and there is no end in sight.

The great numbers of people are using up — at a frightening rate — the riches and irreplaceable resources with which this planet was endowed.

Man pours wastes, chemicals, and other dangerous substances into the earth's streams, lakes, and oceans, befouling them.

He poisons the air with deadly gases and radioactive materials.

He exterminates the creatures of the woods and waters.

In his search for wealth he uproots great forests and makes the earth a wasteland.

God made this planet self-renewing. But so immense is the damage wrought by man that even the patient, healing forces of nature cannot repair it. The life-support systems are strained.

In the blinding smog of pollution, in the contaminated waters, in the ravaged woodlands, is a fearful warning:

If man does not change his ways, he could make the earth a place in which he could no longer live.

Chapter 2
AND GOD MADE THE FIRMAMENT

And God said, Let there be a firmament in the midst of the waters, and let it divide the waters from the waters.

And God made the firmament and divided the waters which were under the firmament from the waters which were above the firmament: and it was so.

And God called the firmament Heaven.

Genesis 1:6-8

God's firmament, the sky, stretches from the earth to the faraway reaches of the universe. Its lowest portion, the atmosphere, extends upward and outward for hundreds of miles. It is an invisible shield, keeping us and our planet from harm.

Few of us realize how magnificently the shield of the atmosphere protects us. Each day a billion fragments of cosmic debris — pieces of stone and metal from outer space — bombard our earth. No sooner do they enter the atmosphere than it sets them on fire and burns them to dust — or it makes them explode in a shower of sparks. These are the meteors and the shooting stars that blaze through our heavens.

Cosmic rays and other dangerous forms of radiation also penetrate our atmosphere. But the atmosphere absorbs and weakens them so they do little damage to life on earth.

The Wondrous Air

The atmosphere supplies us with the air we breathe. What a strange and wondrous thing it is! Take a deep breath now and appreciate the miracle of air. You could live for days and days without food, but not for more than minutes without air.

Most of every breath of air that enters your lungs is made up of gas. Not just one gas, but many. Seventy-eight percent is nitrogen. Another 21 percent is oxygen. What of the other 1 percent? Largely it is argon and carbon dioxide. Tiny fractions of hydrogen, ozone, helium, neon, and other gases are in that breath, too. Water vapor and less desirable things are also in the air — dust, smoke, pollen, and particles of solid matter.

Of all the gases in the air, three are essential to life — nitrogen, oxygen, and carbon dioxide. All the living things on earth — man, plants, and animals — need oxygen to breathe. The proportion of oxygen in the air is very important. The atmosphere of the planet Venus, for example, is 95 percent carbon dioxide and only a fraction of oxygen — not enough to support life as we know it. It is the green plants that make life possible on earth for us and the animals. The plants take carbon dioxide out of the atmosphere and put back oxygen in its place. The air would not keep us alive without green plants.

Winds and Weather

Our atmosphere also helps make the weather. Water vapor — made up of hydrogen and oxygen — rises from our lakes, rivers and seas and forms clouds. From the clouds fall rain, sleet, snow, and hail. The pressure of the atmosphere creates winds in some places, calms in others, storms in others. The atmosphere also keeps our planet warm enough for us to live on. The carbon dioxide in the atmosphere helps to trap the heat that comes from the sun and keeps much of it from being radiated back into space.

Many of the beautiful sights of this earthly paradise are created by the atmosphere — the ruddy glory of the sunset, the many-colored arch of the rainbow, the fleecy flocks of clouds wandering across the blue vault of heaven. In recent years, however, these sights have become harder to see and enjoy in many places. The skies are growing murky and grim — especially in the cities. The air stings our eyes and bites our lungs.

Man, with his machines and smokestacks, has been pouring into the atmosphere heavy clouds of noxious gases, acids, metals, particles, and other harmful substances in enormous quantity, day and night.

Not only has he darkened the heavens. He has made the air in many places perilous to breathe.

The Poisoned Air

The air we breathe is saturated with pollution. The internal combustion engine, which propels our automobiles, is the greatest polluter in history. Do you have any idea of what this mechanical monster is doing to our atmosphere? For every 1,000 gallons of gasoline the automobile engine consumes, it vomits into the air 3,200 pounds of carbon monoxide, a poisonous gas. It releases 200 to 400 pounds of organic vapors, including the hydrocarbons, which are known to cause cancer. It also releases nitrogen oxides, sulfur compounds, leads, acids, and other substances, all of which are harmful.

But the automobile engine produces only half of our air pollution. The other half comes from many other sources: steel mills, public utilities, petroleum refineries, and other industrial installations, as well as heating plants and trash burning.

Experts estimate that every year we release 200 million tons of waste products into the air. That is about a ton for every American!

The air is becoming a cesspool. And what do you suppose that cesspool is doing to our health? As pollution of the air has risen, cases of emphysema, bronchitis, and asthma have all increased dramatically. More and more people are coughing and wheezing their lives away. And those lives are ending earlier.

The Killer Smog

Everyone has heard of smog. Smog occurs when the air is full of smoke and fog. The London smog of December, 1952, was the deadliest ever known to man. The season was exceptionally cold, and Londoners burned a great deal of coal. The air was heavy with sulfur dioxide and other pollutants. The "pea-soup" fog lingered for days, and it penetrated everywhere. Coughing, gasping people filled the hospitals. Weeks after the smog lifted, people were still dying from its effects. The final tally of deaths attributed to the smog was four thousand.

Killer smogs have occurred in Los Angeles, New York, and other cities. In these places, daily reports are issued on the condition of the air, so people who have lung trouble can stay indoors. When the air is very bad, plants that cause pollution are ordered to shut down.

Wanton Waste

Not only people, but growing things also suffer when pollution is severe. In one recent year, California lost half of its citrus crop as a result of air pollution. More than a million ponderosa pines were damaged by air-borne chemicals in the San Bernardino National Forest near Los Angeles. Farms and forests in other states have suffered. For the nation as a whole the annual loss has been estimated at half a billion dollars.

Many priceless art treasures have been damaged by the poisons in the air. In the Boston Museum of Fine Arts hundreds of bronze works of art are blotched with black spots. In a large number of cities, paintings, monuments, statues, valuable books, manuscripts, and the exteriors of historic buildings are suffering.

Year by year, as America grows — puts up more factories and buys more cars — air pollution grows too. If so much damage is being done to our environment and ourselves today, what will it be like in the year 2,000?

To Walk in Darkness

As Harold Laski pointed out: "We must plan our civilization or we must perish."

Perhaps things will be better. The Federal Government now requires late-model automobiles to be equipped to produce less pollution. The Environmental Protection Agency has the power to establish and enforce standards that limit the emission of pollutants by certain types of industrial plants.

But what about older cars? What about the rest of industry?

Recently the Smithsonian Institution made a survey of the amount of sunlight falling on Washington, D.C. It found that direct sunlight had declined 16 percent. The carbon dioxide in the atmosphere had risen 11 percent.

In the beginning, God gave us clean air and sunlight. They are precious gifts.

"To accomplish great things, we must not only act but also to dream, not only to plan but also believe," wrote Anatole France.

What Can Be Done

We can stop wasting our air
    by not open burning heedlessly
    by not letting industrial and private engines idle uselessly
We can stop contaminating the air
    by using low-lead and low-sulphur fuels
    by bagging dust and reducing sprays that permeate the air
    by stopping radio-active discharges
We can start adding to the supply of our air
    by planting green belt areas, trees and shrubs to make oxygen
We can start restoring our air
    by removing carbon dioxide with plant life and auto emission controls.

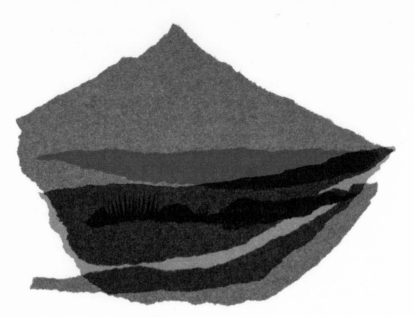

Chapter 3

LET THE DRY LAND APPEAR

And God said, Let the waters under the heaven be gathered together unto one place, and let the dry land appear: and it was so.

And God called the dry land Earth; and the gathering together of the waters called he Seas: and God saw that it was good.

And God said, Let the earth bring forth grass, the herb yielding seed, and the fruit tree yielding fruit after his kind, whose seed is in itself, upon the earth: and it was so.

Genesis 1:9-11

Not Michelangelo, not Rodin, not Saint-Gaudens, nor all the other sculptors that ever lived could have fashioned so great a masterpiece as our earth. For its contrasts of delicate beauty and rugged splendor, for its infinite variety, no work of art can vie with the land on which we live. God made it vast, though not so vast as the waters; the land covers three-tenths of the globe. And He endowed the land with riches and resources beyond imagining, but not without limit.

Each of the regions of the earth God made different, as though He wished man to have a habitation of which he would never tire. In the north He placed the glittering land of ice and snow, and next to it the dark tundra, where the hardy moss and lichen grow and the caribou follows its age-old trails. Southward the frozen plain gives way to great evergreen forests, and then to the oak, maple, birch, and other trees that shed their leaves when autumn comes.

Further south He placed the hot, bright deserts, with shifting sands that cover one-fifth of the land; here God gave the plants tough skins, like the cactus, so that they could endure the heat. And He made the tropical rainforest, the grass-covered prairies, the rocky shore, and other places wonderful beyond description. To each He gave plants and animals suited to it and to each other.

"The land is our mother," the American Indians said. And they loved their mother, for she was good to them, giving them of her bounty — beans and corn, buffalo, elk, deer, and beaver, and cotton-wood bark for their ponies to chew. Of her gifts the Indians took only what they needed. They killed not for sport or blood lust, but to satisfy their need for food and shelter.

As Stewart Lee Udall explained in his book, *The Quiet Crisis:* "The most common trait of all primitive peoples is a reverence for the life-giving earth, and the native American shared this elemental ethic: the land was alive to his loving touch, and he, its son, was brother to all creatures. His feelings were made visible in medicine bundles and dance rhythms for rain, and all of his religious rites and land attitudes savored the inseparable world of nature and God, the master of Life. During the long Indian tenure the land remained undefiled save for scars no deeper than the scratches of cornfield clearings or the farming canals of the Hohokams on the Arizona desert."

Threat to the Land

Like people around the world who live close to nature, the Indians had the wisdom to know that they belonged to the earth. But not the men from Europe. They held that the earth belonged to them — and they used it and abused it to enrich themselves.

Cattle were in demand, so the men covered the grasslands with cattle. In time the animals cropped the land bare, leaving the topsoil naked to the wind. Wheat was in demand, and cotton, so planters sowed millions of acres with each of these crops. When the earth was exhausted, they did not seek to renew or restore it, but moved onward. Where there was little rainfall the soil turned to dust. And no one cared.

Do you remember the "dust bowl" of the 1930s? Strong winds blew across large areas of the prairie states, raising the dust in vast, dense waves. Up and away the dust was carried. When the winds died down, the dust fell to the ground. It settled upon good growing crops and rich grasslands. They suffocated. They were destroyed.

In May, 1934, one of the worst dust storms of all time took place. A gigantic cloud of dust particles — experts say it contained 300 million tons of topsoil — was lifted up and spread over half the United States. In New York City, for five hours the dust veiled the sun. In the middle of the day, people had to turn on their lights.

That great cloud was a warning. And men responded to it. They suddenly saw that they must renew and strengthen the earth. They planted grass and forests to hold the moisture in the land and keep the soil from blowing away again.

Fiona Macleod wrote:

> "A handful of pine-seed will cover mountains
> with the green majesty of forest.
> I too will set my face to the wind
> and throw my handful of seed on high."

But in many other places they continued — and they still continue — to lay waste the environment. Shopping centers rise where yesterday nature's self-restoring wilderness stood. Careless building developers cut down trees and scrape away grass, which God put there to hold water. Now, when the heavy rains fall, communities are inundated by floods.

A society of superconsumers, we make few things that last. We prefer to buy anew rather than reuse. Abandoned automobiles, beer cans, pop bottles, plastic containers are everywhere.

It is ugly. It is wasteful. It is not the natural way of God.

"The greatest domestic problem facing our country is saving our soil and water. Our soil belongs also to unborn generations." Sam Rayburn declared.

Lunar Landscapes

We obtain 40 percent of our coal by strip mining. In many areas, coal beds lie near the surface, and the mine operators strip away the beautiful forests and meadows covering them to gouge out the coal. No place is spared if its owner needs money.

In Belmont County, Ohio, some time ago, a local historian reported that an unmarked Quaker graveyard had been leased to the strippers. In it lay the remains of William Milhous, Sr., and Jr., President Richard Milhous Nixon's great-great-great-grandfather and his great-great-grandfather.

"It seems like no one cares," the historian said sadly.

And so, in one region and another, an area as large as the state of Delaware has been ripped bare. One and one-half million acres, torn up by the giant shovels. Today, many states require the mine operators to reclaim and replant the land. So should every state — and they should see to it that the damage is conscientiously repaired.

Do not think that the United States is the only country that allows its land to be stripped. Russia gets much of its coal and manganese by strip mining. Large areas are devastated. The region where one mine is located has been turned into a "lunar landscape," Russian conservationists complain.

Nature's Holy Places

In our national parks and wildlife preserves we try to keep alive for our children some memory of what this great land was once like. In the wilderness we can find health and a profound sense of peace. "The thunderous silence of deep canyons, the solitude of high mountains, the luminosity of deserts," declares Rene Dubos, a famed biologist, keeps us "in resonance with cosmic events." Yet man, in his greed, constantly harasses or seeks to despoil nature's holy places.

In Florida, where there is a great demand for land, new communities are constantly being constructed. To aid these projects, the Army Corps of Engineers built canals through the wild preserve of the Everglades and regulated the flow of water. This helped the projects but not the preserve. Denied sufficient water, many of the Everglades' creatures died of thirst. The number of wading birds, for example, fell from 1.5 million to fewer than 50,000. Fires consumed half a million acres.

Only after conservationists raised their voices loudly did the Army agree to change its practices.

In this true story there is a lesson. Shout — do not whisper — if you would be heard in nature's cause.

Abraham Lincoln once said: "Die when I may, I want it said of me by those who knew me best, that I always plucked a thistle and planted a flower where I thought a flower should grow."

Strange Viands

Not only is God's good green earth being placed in jeopardy by man's greed or thoughtlessness — our own bodies may be, too. Farmers, in order to bring more food crops to market, use large quantities of pesticides to control the insects that prey upon them. The pesticides are blown everywhere, and they coat the fodder eaten by cattle and other livestock raised for the market. The animals also are given antibiotics to keep them healthy. These alien substances are stored in their bodies. When we eat the meat from these animals, we transfer the substances to our own tissues.

We store many other unwanted, unneeded substances in our bodies. Today, food processors and manufacturers put a lengthy list of chemicals into their packaged products to make them easier to prepare, to make them look better and taste better, and to lengthen their "shelf life." At present there are some 2,500 of these chemicals — called "food additives" — and more are being developed all the time. Some are used in almost every kind of packaged food.

When you bite into an ordinary slice of "boughten" bread and butter you are getting many of these additives. Magnesium oxide, coal tar, nordihydroguaiaretic acid (can you pronounce it?), polyoxyethylene esters, monocalcium phosphate, sodium propionate, and chlorine dioxide are just some of the possibilities.

How safe are the food additives? It is the duty of the United States Food and Drug Administration to check the wholesomeness of our foods. To date the agency has tested only half of these chemicals. We have only ourselves to blame. We do not give the Food and Drug Administration enough money and men to conduct the proper tests. This might be another good matter to shout, not whisper, about.

Do you remember the furore when cyclamates were banned in 1969? At that time they had been in use for nineteen years as artificial sweeteners. Finally the evidence was so overwhelming that cyclamates produced cancer in test animals that the government had to prohibit the use of the sweetener. Many other additives employed in everyday food products are suspected of being dangerous to people. Meanwhile we go on eating them.

We cannot afford to gamble with the future of the earth — and we must not gamble with our own health!

What Can Be Done

We can stop wasting our land
>by preventing deforestation and stop stripping top soil
>by preventing erosion with flood controls
>by supporting programs and legislation that prevent depletion of land

We can stop ruining our land
>by not strip-mining
>by not over-grazing and over-farming
>by preventing forest fires
>by not dumping waste
>by not covering the land with concrete

We can start adding to our land supply
>by protecting shore lines
>by reclaiming unproductive land
>by setting aside parklands and forest preserves

We can start cleaning and restoring our land
>by cleaning up dumps
>by recycling everything
>by protecting the soil with ground cover
>by reforestation
>by making ponds and lakes

Chapter 4

LET THERE BE LIGHT

And God said, Let there be lights in the firmament of the heaven to divide the day from the night; and let them be for signs, and for seasons, and for days, and years:

And let them be for lights in the firmament of the heaven to give light upon the earth: and it was so.

And God made two great lights; the greater light to rule the day, and the lesser light to rule the night: he made the stars also.

And God set them in the firmament of the heaven to give light upon the earth.

Genesis 1:14-17

The sun, which rules the day, is a vast fiery ball of luminous gas. It is so huge that we could put a million planets the size of our earth into the space it occupies — and still have room for hundreds of thousands more.

The giant of our solar system, the sun holds the earth, the moon, and the other planets in their courses with the invisible strength of gravity. They travel around the sun in their orbits in perfect rhythm, like the cogs of a heavenly watch.

Energy, heat, light — God set the sun in the sky to give us these blessings. Without the sun the moon would be dark — its light is but the pale reflection of the radiance of the sun. The great burning ball is hotter than we can easily conceive. On its blazing surface, where the flames lash upward for many miles, the temperature is 6,000 degrees centigrade — hotter than the hottest fire on earth. A lesser fire would not suffice. To reach us, the sun's rays must travel a great distance — 93 million miles — across the abyss of space.

Without the sun, life as we know it would be impossible. The earth would be a dark, cold, forbidding place. Small wonder that the people of ancient Egypt, Mexico, and other lands worshipped the sun as a god and made sacrifices to it. To them it seemed to be reborn every morning, and they hailed the sunrise with hosannas of joy. Even today the sun and sunshine are symbols of joy and happiness to us.

The Energy of the Sun

We thank the Lord for our daily bread, but we little think how He uses the sun to provide it for us. The sun sends rays of energy to the earth. On our planet, God gave the green plant alone the secret knowledge of how to capture the sun's energy, store it up, and use it to make sugar, the basic food of nature, on which all life depends. Green is truly the color of nature. The green plant and the sun made Eden possible on earth.

The green plant works its miracle by photosynthesis. This word comes from the Greek for "putting together with light." In the plant's green leaves is a mysterious substance called chlorophyll. The chlorophyll captures the radiance of the sun and blends it with elements from the water, the soil, and the air. The miraculous sugar it makes with them — nature's manna — it uses to grow on. It stores the sun's radiance in its tissues. When the animals eat green plants they transfer the sun's energy to their own bodies. When we eat fruit, vegetables, and meat, we also are taking into our bodies some of that wonderful energy from outer space to use and to store for future use.

Fire from the Sun

Have you ever put a match to logs in a fireplace? When you do, they flare up brightly. They give off intense heat. That light and heat are the energy of the sun, which was stored up by the tree from which the logs came. For tens of years, or even hundreds, the tree was gathering that energy and locking it in its tissues.

When we burn coal and oil, they give us warmth, light, and power that traveled through space to the earth in the rays of the sun millions and millions of years ago. These fuels are brought up from under the ground, but once they were on the surface. Once they were plants in vast green swamps that covered the land in prehistoric times. Over the ages the earth buried the swamp plants, and over aeons of time they changed into their present form. Because coal and oil come from fossil plants we call them "fossil fuels."

The fire that creates all of this energy — the fire that burns on the sun — is no ordinary blaze. It is atomic energy. Long before man discovered fire on the earth, the sun was splitting hydrogen atoms and releasing their energy. Because the sun is so huge, its supply of atoms and energy will last for billions of years.

Will mankind last as long?

The Power of the Atom

In a speech, Adlai Stevenson said: "Nature is neutral. Man has wrested from nature the power to make the world a desert or to make deserts bloom. There is no evil in the atom; only in men's souls."

In 1945 men detonated the first atomic bombs. These unique instruments of destruction took tens of thousands of human lives. For many years afterward we continued to build and test atomic weapons of greater deadliness. We stopped testing on the earth's surface in 1963 when our scientists discovered that radioactive fallout from the atomic explosions was permeating the air, land, and waters of the earth. Radioactive substances such as strontium 90 were building up in our food. Babies were absorbing them in their mothers' milk. Radioactive materials were lodged in their bones. In minute quantities, to be sure. But still they were there.

The power of the atom is awesome. Foolhardy man was using that power before he understood what it was and what it could do. Even today, atomic scientists freely admit they have much to learn about it.

Still, we are using the power of the atom on a wider and wider scale.

At the present time, in the United States alone, we have 150 nuclear power plants in the planning or operating stage. Hundreds more will be built before the end of the century. The Atomic Energy Commission tells us that the plants in operation are quite safe — but reports show they have released traces of radioactive elements into the air and water. Zinc 65, one of these elements, has been found in algae and in fish in the vicinity of one nuclear plant. The Atomic Energy Commission has tightened its overall regulations — but concerned scientists say they should be tighter still. Radioactive substances kill if taken in large doses. But even in small doses they can cause cancer, sterility, anemia, and other diseases. The Environmental Protective Agency declares that "radioactivity has implications for human health which science has hardly begun to explore."

We are confronted by other dangers from our atomic power plants. Their wastes remain radioactive for thousands of years (astonishing but true!) and are so potent they must be buried in deserts or deep under the ground. Sometimes the wastes leak out of the tanks in which they are stored. Within the nuclear power reactors themselves, there is always a chance that a pipe may break. The government assures us this will not happen. But the more nuclear power plants we have, the more the odds tend to shift against us. And what if there were an earthquake?

Atomic energy is a force more powerful than dynamite or TNT. "Make haste slowly" was a proverb of the ancients. We would face fewer risks from this new source of energy if we did not rush ahead with it so fast.

We should take time to study the problems of atomic energy and its threat to the environment and human life before we become involved with it too deeply.

Later it may be too late.

Already the energy crisis is creating drastic changes all over the world. Airline schedules have been cut sharply. Because of the gasoline shortage, automobile speed has been reduced to 55 miles per hour and, in some countries, driving on Sundays has been banned.

Thermostats are being turned back in homes and businesses. Lack of fuel for factories and utilities is reducing output.

Lights are being dimmed or turned out entirely in some instances.

Schools are shortening terms for the winter months to save fuel, and we have year round daylight savings time.

And no one can say what other measures will be required before our needs for energy are brought into line with the available supply.

What Can Be Done

We can stop wasting our energy
    by not wasting electricity
    by not wasting gasoline and other fuels
We can stop blocking out our sunlight
    by not fouling the air with chemicals, dust, metals, gases
We can start adding to our energy
    by burning garbage and trash for fuel
    by developing safe atomic generation
    by using water power such as the tides
We can start using clean energy sources
    by using electric power for transportation
    by using clean atomic power
    by using clean fuels low in sulphur and other noxious elements.

Chapter 5

LET THE WATERS
BE GATHERED TOGETHER

And God said, Let the waters bring forth abundantly the moving creature that hath life, and fowl that may fly above the earth in the open firmament of heaven.

And God created great whales, and every living creature that moveth, which the waters brought forth abundantly, after their kind, and every winged fowl after his kind: and God saw that it was good.

And God blessed them, saying, Be fruitful, and multiply, and fill the waters in the seas, and let fowl multiply in the earth.

Genesis 1:20-22

Water is a magic elixir. We could not live long without it — nor could any other thing that has life. Water makes up most of our blood and our flesh. It makes up most of the sap and the tissue of plants.

Thank God there is so much water! It covers about 70 percent of the earth. Only 1 percent is fresh water — all the rest is salt. Yet all the birds and beasts and the plants of the land depend on this 1 percent of fresh water for life.

Water is always going or coming. It rises into the air as vapor, from our oceans, lakes, rivers, and streams, and forms clouds. The clouds drift over the earth. When the vapor cools, it forms drops and falls as rain. The rain refreshes the land and fills the lakes and streams. Then the water flows back to the oceans or changes into vapor, and the cycle begins anew.

Rachel Carson, in *The Sea Around Us,* said:

"The sea lies all around us. The commerce of all lands must cross it. The very winds that move over the lands have been cradled on its broad expanse and seek ever to return to it. The continents themselves dissolve and pass to the sea, in grain after grain of eroded land . . . In its mysterious past it encompasses all the dim origins of life and receives in the end, after, it may be, many transmutations, the dead husks of that same life. For all at last returns to the sea — the beginning and the end."

Salty though the ocean water is, it teems with life. It has creatures of every size and form, from the tiny goby — less than half an inch long — to the great whale, which is over a hundred feet. Fishes with all the colors of the rainbow dart through tropical waters. Plants, too, like algae and plankton, abound. Many are so tiny we need a magnifying lens to see them. Yet there are such unbelievably vast quantities of them that they make 70 percent of the oxygen in the atmosphere, by the miraculous food producing process of photosynthesis. The fishes feed on the algae and plankton and on each other. It is a varied, lively, wonderful world, the world of the waters, in which every kind of living thing depends for its existence on the things around it.

"When I would beget content and increase confidence in the power and wisdom and providence of Almighty God," declared Izaak Walton, "I will walk the meadows by some gliding stream, and there contemplate the lilies that take no care, and those very many other little living creatures that are not only created, but fed (man knows not how) by the goodness of the God of Nature, and therefore trust in Him."

But strange and fearful things have been happening to our waters, from the smallest pond to the greatest ocean.

Our Waters in Trouble

Some years ago the explorer Thor Heyerdahl made a voyage across the Atlantic in a small boat. Sailing close to the surface, he was able to see things that ordinary ocean travelers do not. In the midst of the ocean, hundreds and hundreds of miles from land, he found great solid globs of oil. He sailed through a muddle of refuse of every description, including garbage, plastic containers, and squeeze tubes.

How did that rubbish get so far out in the ocean? There was too much of it for to have been thrown overboard by ocean liners, though they contributed. Most of it came from shore. Each year, thousands of barges pull out from the land, loaded with immense quantities of solid waste. After they have traveled three miles from land, they are free to discharge their cargo. And discharge it they do — to the extent of about five hundred pounds annually for every American!

Industrial plants contribute more than their share to water pollution. They discharge their wastes directly into the ocean, or into our lakes and rivers by way of city sewers. Sulfuric acid, cyanide, zinc, benzine, fertilizers, pesticides are only a few of the contaminants that have been found in our land and ocean waters. In a recent study, the Scripps Institution of Oceanography at La Jolla, California, reported that almost all of the fish in the ocean carried DDT in their tissues. The level of lead in the water was over seven times what it is naturally. The institution also reported the water showed traces of radioactivity produced by man. (Not enough to kill — but nothing to feel easy about.)

But all of this is only a small part of the spreading blight of pollution in our waters. Every year, oil tankers collide or run aground, spilling millions of gallons of bunker oil. Our energy-hungry society drills oil wells offshore, and every so often one of them has a blowout, shooting great amounts of oil into the water. Each year, more than seventy-five hundred cases of oil pollution occur. The slick spreads for hundreds of square miles, coating the feathers of countless marine birds and causing their death. Millions of fish are poisoned. The damage to water plants is incalculable. Beaches are ruined, and so is the shore life they support.

Not only in America. We might suppose that Russia, which rules its economy and its people with an iron will, would not have any water pollution problems. But human carelessness and lack of foresight are without national boundaries. Soviet fishermen report that their sturgeon catch has been decreasing in the Caspian Sea, and some kinds of fish are dying out altogether. The Caspian is surrounded by oil wells, and oil is always draining into it.

The Menace of Mercury

The oil industry has been made aware of its responsibility in polluting our waters. Other industries received a warning that they were exposing the environment and human life to danger in 1970, when mercury was found in fish taken from Lake St. Clair. Industry uses mercury in paper, paint, insecticides, and other common products. If introduced into the body in sufficient quantity, this element can cause blindness, brain damage, and death.

The United States Government estimated that 250 tons of mercury were being discharged into the Great Lakes annually. A flurry of tests showed that mercury was present in fish and game birds in many of our states, and in swordfish and tuna caught in the Pacific Ocean. Overnight, these two kinds of fish disappeared from our store counters.

Frequently, we have the laws to protect us against a danger like this, but we rarely bother to enforce them. After the mercury scare, President Richard M. Nixon announced that an 1899 act that prohibits the discharge of industrial wastes into navigable waterways without a special permit would be strictly enforced. Within a year, mercury discharges were greatly reduced.

Poisoned Lakes and Rivers

Henry David Thoreau said, "A lake is the landscape's most beautiful and expressive feature. It is earth's eye, looking into which the beholder measures the depth of his own nature."

Did you know that many American communities (thirteen hundred of them in 1971) have been pouring human sewage into bodies of water nearby without any treatment at all? Many other cities discharge their wastes with just a minimum of treatment. The Hudson River alone receives the sewage of over ten million people. Lake Erie also receives enormous quantities of human waste. Beaches along both bodies of water have had to be closed because of the dangerous pollution.

Of other wastes poured into our waters, detergents are among the commonest. Many contain phosphates, which are, incidentally, a plant food. The phosphates and other nutrients in our sewage stimulate the overgrowth of water plants — a process called eutrophication — and this upsets the ecological balance. After a while the plants are so abundant that they blanket the lakes and streams. They decay, and the oxygen in the water is used up. The fish die of suffocation. The body of water turns into a foul-smelling bog. Over a third of our hundred thousand lakes suffer from some degree of eutrophication. Once-beautiful Lake Erie is the most tragic example.

More than sixty years ago, Theodore Roosevelt tried to launch a campaign to make the water of Lake Erie good enough to drink. "You can't get pure water and put sewage into the lake," he told the public. But few were listening. Only when this enormous lake had been turned into a malodorous swamp did the public and industry begin to wake up.

Today, government is doing things to keep our waters clean. Federal funds are helping cities to build or improve municipal sewage treatment plants. Local governments are starting to play an active role. But it is no more than a beginning. Only a small fraction of the money and attention needed to prevent the pollution of our waters is being given.

"There is scarcely a stream," states the Environmental Protection Agency, "that does not bear some mark of man's abuse. The list of 'most polluted' rivers spans the continent."

What Can Be Done

We can stop wasting water
> by careful use in industry, home and business
> by repairing leaking plumbing and equipment

We can stop contaminating our water
> by not dumping garbage, sewage and poisons into it
> by using biodegradable cleansers

We cannot add to our supply of water, but we can conserve and better use the water we have
> by cleaning polluted water through purification centers
> by recycling the water used
> by stocking rivers and lakes with fish

Chapter 6

CATTLE AND CREEPING THING

And God said, Let the earth bring forth the living creature after his own kind, cattle, and creeping thing, and beast of the earth after his kind: and it was so.

And God made the beast of the earth after his kind, and cattle after their kind, and everything that creepeth upon the earth after his kind: and God saw that it was good.

Genesis 1:24, 25

The creatures that God fashioned on the land are strange and wonderful to behold. He made animals fitted to dwell in every nook and cranny of the earth — in the deserts, the mountains, the forests, the plains. To each creature He gave special gifts to help it in its struggle for life. To the giraffe He gave a long neck, so it can reach the leaves on the uppermost branches of trees when those lower down are gone. To the turtle He gave a tough shell beneath which it can hide if danger threatens. To the bear He gave the power to sleep away the long hungry winter. To the honeybee He gave a sting to keep its foes at a distance while it carries its nectar home to the hive.

The world of God's animals is a world of miracles great and small.

Charles Darwin wrote: "The plow is one of the most ancient and most valuable of man's inventions, but long before he existed the land in fact was regularly plowed and still continues to be thus plowed by earthworms. It may be doubted whether there are many other animals which have played so important a part in the history of the world, as have these lowly organized creatures."

The Balance of Nature

Each thing in nature has its life interwoven with the lives of the things around it. They live in a delicate balance — the balance of nature. This balance is never completely at rest. It keeps shifting.

Suppose, for example, the warm days of spring come early one year. The insects hatch quickly, and more of them live. That year the multitude of creeping, crawling things is greater than usual — out of proportion to other creatures. Birds feed on insects, and because they have more than enough to eat they prosper; more of them mate and have families. As the birds increase, they consume more and more of the insects. Now, suddenly, there are too many birds for the dwindling food supply. Some must go hungry and perish. Sometimes, if the numbers of a species are too great and they live too close together, disease breaks out among them, sharply reducing their numbers. Nature always seeks an equilibrium among its creatures.

The balance of nature has seesawed back and forth in this way for millions of years. In recent times, however, it has begun to lean crazily in one direction. For man has laid his hand heavily on one side of the scale and each year he presses harder. He has leveled forests, destroying the homes of many kinds of animals. He has covered millions of once-green acres with concrete parking lots. He has tampered with nature's balance in a hundred other ways without giving a thought to the consequences.

Examples? Here is one out of many. Some years ago the graceful elm tree was smitten by a disease. The infection was carried from one tree to another by an insect, and great numbers of trees died. To

33

combat the disease, tree experts sprayed the elms with an insecticide called DDT. Confidently the experts asserted that DDT would not harm birds — only insects.

Then a strange thing happened. In the region where the elms had been sprayed, it was noticed that the robins, once so abundant, had disappeared. Or else people stumbled over their bodies, frozen in death. In some parts of the region, 86 percent of the birds died. Of those that lived, many could not lay eggs the next spring.

What misfortune had befalled the robins? Examination revealed that they contained DDT in their tissues. The spray, it was true, had been advertised as not harmful to birds. But, to quote a great ecologist, Barry Commoner, "everything goes somewhere." The insecticide had coated the leaves of the elms. In the autumn the leaves covered the ground in deep layers. Earthworms burrowed through them and dined on the deadly leaves. Then the robins came, searching for food, and gobbled the poisoned worms. A dozen worms carried enough DDT to kill a robin — and each robin ate dozens of worms!

Many other kinds of birds were struck down by the poison. With the birds cut down in number, the insects that they usually fed upon multiplied without check. Nature's balance had been upset, and soon the insects overwhelmed the region. Many grew immune to pesticides, and new and deadlier ones had to be invented.

In *Silent Spring*, Rachel Carson wrote: "Over increasingly large areas of the United States, spring now comes unheralded by the return of the birds, and the early mornings are strangely silent where once they were filled with the beauty of bird song."

And what of man? Sprays intended for insects have found their way into the water we drink, the food we eat. "The average American," declares the Environmental Protection Agency, "now carries 12 parts per million of DDT in his fatty tissue." There is no "direct evidence" that this quantity is dangerous — yet. But "misuse of various pesticides is implicated in up to 200 human deaths per year and thousands of cases of severe illness."

Endangered Species

Pesticides are not the only threat to the animals. Once the commonest form of wildlife on this continent was the passenger pigeon. In 1810 a naturalist reported one flock of these birds that was a mile wide — and 240 miles long! But the birds were easy to kill and tasty to eat. Hunters slew them in great numbers and builders leveled the woodlands where they lived. Out of an estimated 5 billion passenger pigeons not a single one remains alive today.

The buffalo (which once numbered perhaps 100 million) has almost followed the passenger pigeon to extinction. Four hundred different kinds of birds and mammals have disappeared forever in the last one hundred years. Hundreds of other animals are endangered — the sea cow, whooping crane, ivory-billed woodpecker, fur seal, peregrine falcon, blue whale, and key deer among them. The Government now tries to protect these species, but at every turn the survival of other creatures is threatened. Why? Because man kills them for sport or profit, or bulldozes down their native woodlands.

Beatrix Potter in *The Journal of Beatrix Potter* remarked: "Why do some people talk with such assurance about what they are going to do with the world, as though they owned it when really our share is such a small one? Birds and butterflies, bees and flying insects fill the air; tiny animals climb and burrow and scuttle. And underneath the ground a whole world of life goes on that we never see — moles with grey velvet coats push along, their strong front feet swinging through the earth with a swimmer's breast stroke. Behind them come the ground-mice on sly, flying feet, and tucked under a stone is a grey worm, rolled up for winter. There is myriad life under, on, and above the earth."

All of life is interwoven. Animals do more than add beauty and interest to our world. They are part of the web of life, in which every part depends upon those around it. If we make it impossible for them to live, we may be making it impossible for ourselves as well.

A little over a hundred years ago, Charles Darwin observed: "It is interesting to contemplate an entangled bank, clothed with many plants of many kinds, with birds singing on the bushes, with various insects flitting about, and with worms crawling through the damp earth, and to reflect that these elaborately constructed forms, so different from each other, and dependent on each other in so complex a manner, have all been produced by laws acting around us."

And nearly four hundred years ago, Montaigne wisely advised: "Let us permit nature to have her way: she understands her business better than we do."

We can no longer ignore the warning that we must preserve the life around us.

What Can Be Done

We can stop wasting our wildlife
    by preserving their natural habitats
    by not hunting them for fun
    by not over-killing them for food
We can stop destroying our wildlife
    by not using DDT and other chemicals that kill
    by not exterminating living creatures
We can start adding to our wildlife
    by creating wildlife refuges and bird sanctuaries
    by stocking streams and lakes with fish
    by feeding and caring for them in their natural environments
We can start restoring our wildlife
    by regenerating species
    by animal husbandry
    by breeding for release into natural habitats

Chapter 7

BE FRUITFULL AND MULTIPLY

And God said, Let us make man in our image, after our likeness: and let them have dominion over the fish of the sea, and over the fowl of the air, and over the cattle, and over all the earth, and over every creeping thing that creepeth upon the earth.

So God created man in his own image, in the image of God created he him; male and female created he them.

And God blessed them, and God said unto them, Be fruitful and multiply, and replenish the earth, and subdue it . . .

Genesis 1:26-28

Many of God's commandments we have ignored or broken, but one we have obeyed with great faithfulness: Be fruitful and multiply. From the first man and woman He made in the beginning, incredible multitudes have descended.

Today over 3.5 billion of us are spread over the earth. Each year, 72 million more souls join us.

When man was new upon the earth, his numbers were few. One could travel for hundreds of miles without seeing another human being. Only endless plains, forests, and mountains, teeming with the wildlife with which God had stocked them.

It was the men and women of that earlier, emptier world that the Lord charged to be fruitful and multiply.

A million years and more passed. Each year almost as many died as were born, for in those faraway times doctors knew little about how to cure the ailing. But slowly the population grew. Grew and grew.

When the Lord Jesus came into the world, it had perhaps 250 million inhabitants. If you walked a square mile you would find no more than six people.

How Many People?

Thomas Robert Malthus stated: "Population, when unchecked, increases in a geometrical ratio. Subsistence increases only in an arithmetical ratio. A slight acquaintance with numbers will show the immensity of the first power in comparison of the second."

Gradually the population increased. Study these dates and figures to see how it grew:

A.D. 1	250 million	1850	1 billion	1970	3.5 billion
1650	500 million	1930	2 billion		

Do you notice anything curious about the rate of increase? After the birth of Jesus it took over sixteen hundred years for the earth's population to double. But it took only two hundred years for it to double again. Next it took no more than eighty years. And only forty years later, in 1970, the world population had almost doubled again.

Still the numbers keep increasing — and the doubling time keeps getting shorter — as medical science makes it possible for more people to live longer. In the year 2,000, population experts tell us, there will be about 7 billion people on earth. For every square mile, 125 persons.

Do we dare to look beyond that date? The statisticians have already done so.

They tell us that if man continues to multiply at his present rate — and every year there are more of us to multiply — in

38

nine hundred years the earth's population will be 60 million billion (60,000,000,000,000,000) people.

The number is so vast it is unthinkable.

How many people would there be to the square mile? Rather ask: to the square foot. The answer is: *eleven to every square foot of the earth (including the oceans)!*

The Hungry Millions

At this very moment the world has a greater population than it can adequately support. Nine-tenths of the earth's surface is ocean, desert, rock — land that cannot bear crops. Even the most wonderful fertilizers and farming techniques cannot make the remaining one-tenth bring forth enough food to fill the stomachs of the teeming billions.

Tonight, half of the men, women, and children on earth will go to bed hungry. Tomorrow, ten thousand of these will not stir again. They will have died of malnutrition and starvation.

Even as you read this sentence, five human beings — most of them helpless, innocent children — have starved to death.

Hungry children who are far away do not seem very real. They are only abstractions, cold statistics. But if one of these little ones were in the same room with you, great eyes shining in a thin, drawn face, you could not help but feel: something is amiss in God's world. And you would hasten to help.

At the very moment that these five unfortunates are dying of starvation, forty new babies are coming into the world. Forty more mouths to feed — when half of their brothers and sisters do not have enough to eat.

Would it not be more humane that some of these children should not be born than that they should have to face the agonies of starvation?

The Four Horsemen

Already the Four Horsemen of the Apocalypse are riding across the darkening skies. Death and Starvation we have spoken of — but with them ride their equally grim companions, Pestilence and War.

In underdeveloped countries, people live in unbelievable squalor. Sanitation is primitive and medical care is inadequate. Plagues are always breaking out. As the population grows and grows, worse plagues can be predicted.

When people are packed close together and they do not have enough resources or food, they cast jealous glances at the possessions of their neighbors. Why else did Adolf Hitler and his allies plunge us into the most devastating war of all time? Why else are the swarming countries of the world always at each other's throats?

More and more countries are learning how to produce the atomic bomb. The A-bomb is the deadliest weapon ever devised by man. If a war breaks out between the "haves" and the "have-nots" the "A" in A-bomb may no longer stand for "atomic" but for "Armageddon."

But man can take heed and control his numbers while there is still time.

Lands of Abundance

In developed lands like the United States the population grows much more slowly than in underdeveloped countries. Yet even in this broad and bountiful land there seem to be too many of us for our resources. Seventy percent of us are jammed tightly together upon 2 percent of our territory. Many of us go hungry or suffer from malnutrition, while many others enjoy a standard of living without equal in the history of mankind.

But at what a cost! To maintain our standard of living — and because there are so many of us — we are exhausting at a fantastic rate the resources not only of our own country but of every other one that will have dealings with us. Americans represent no more than 6 percent of the population of the globe — yet we are responsible for *35 percent* of the annual consumption of the earth's unrenewable resources.

In the beginning God laid up on this planet enough silver, gold, iron, tin, copper, and other valuable metals and materials to last for all time — if we used them thriftily. Mankind, however, like the Prodigal Son, spends this priceless heritage as though there were no tomorrow. In 150 years or so our fossil fuels — coal and oil — will probably all be gone. We shall have to rely heavily on atomic power. Who can be sure there will be enough of it to satisfy the needs of the entire world? Or that it will be used with safety on such a wide scale?

In our affluent society, our industrial leaders are always discovering new ways to use up more of the earth's limited resources. They are always urging us to buy more — and we do buy. The average American family carries home so many products every year that we are told

$500 of its income must go just to pay for the bags, containers, and cartons they come in.

Can you imagine how many forests are cut down annually to produce the paper, cardboard, and wood that we use? Proudly the Weyerhaeuser Company — a great producer of lumber and lumber products — tells us that in a single year our country uses up so many big trees that with them we could build a boardwalk ten feet wide around the equator *thirty times*. The devastated woodlands are reseeded, of course — but it takes many and many a year to regrow a forest giant.

Robert Frost wrote:

"I wonder about trees:
Why do we wish to bear
Forever the noise of these
More than another noise
So close to our dwelling place?"

Ugly Cities

And all the time there are fewer places for trees to grow in. As the population increases, so do our cities, which spread further and further over the green countryside. For spread they must; the great new numbers of people need places to live and work, and they find them in the cities.

Like giant monsters the cities stretch out their tentacles of concrete toward one another until they meet and merge. Thousands and thousands of miles of dirty concrete, gasoline stations, billboards, diners — where once there were green hills, tall trees, whispering brooks. It is hard to tell where one city ends and another begins.

Every year more and more people are packed into these cities. The fortunate ones live in elegant boxes of brick and glass piled one upon the other. When the people venture out their lungs are invaded by corrosive fumes from the exhausts of thousands of automobiles and trucks. Their ears are deafened by the din of the pneumatic drill, the bus, the airplane.

As Byron expressed it:

"I live not in myself, but I become
Portion of that around me: and to me
High mountains are a feeling, but the hum
Of human cities torture."

Other city dwellers live in ugly, rundown tenement houses. The lots between the buildings are covered with rubble and trash. Packs of half-wild dogs roam the streets. Crime and drug addiction are everywhere. Some of the houses have been abandoned by their owners. Still the poor and the desperate live in them, for they have nowhere else to go — in the greatest and richest land that ever the sun has shone upon.

The men who govern the metropolises know they are ailing. They have drawn up noble plans to tear down the slums — to raise, in their place, attractive, small housing units, where there will be room enough for all, with parks, playgrounds, open space. They have programs to educate and train the poor to raise their standard of living. But plans and programs cost money — huge sums of money. So long as the population keeps growing, the need will always increase faster than the means to take care of it.

Our land, our air, our water are polluted. But do not our troubles with pollution grow from the most basic trouble of all — too many people?

Pollution is a warning — a warning from the Almighty. He is telling us that the earth has only room and resources for so many of us — and no more.

If we limit our numbers, there can be enough of everything for each person on earth.

What Can Be Done

We can stop wasting our population
    by wanton killing and warfare
    by preventing starvation
We can stop ruining our population
    by wiping out chronic endemic diseases
    by improving nutrition
We can add to our population only in direct proportion to adequate supplies of food, land and other necessities of life
We can start rehabilitating our population
    by developing new food resoruces
    by developing land for agriculture and living
    by providing sanitary, healthy living conditions

Chapter 8
DOMINION OVER ALL

. . . (God said) and have dominion over the fish of the sea, and over the fowl of the air, and over every living thing that moveth upon the earth.

And God said, Behold, I have given you every herb bearing seed, which is upon the face of all the earth, and every tree, in the which is the fruit of a tree yielding seed; to you it shall be for meat.

And to every beast of the earth, and to every fowl of the air, and to every thing that creepeth upon the earth, wherein there is life, I have given every green herb for meat: and it was so.

Genesis 1:28-30

The Lord placed in our hands dominion over the entire world and everything within it. He entrusted us with the care of the only planet in the universe on which life is known to exist.

On that wondrous planet, we have seen, everything depends on the things around it. The green plant depends on the earth and sun and the rain; the animal depends upon the green plant and on other animals; and man depends on both.

In the beginning man took from the earth no more of its goodly things than he needed. He allowed the earth time to renew itself and replace what he had taken.

But in the eighteenth century the way man lived and worked began to undergo great changes in the Western world. The most profound of these changes we call the Industrial Revolution. Man made inventions like the cotton gin, the steam engine, the power loom. He even invented machines that made machines. The quiet, peaceful life of earlier times was left behind. In its place came hustle, rush, worry.

The new age of the machine ushered in an age of abundance. Man's numbers multiplied. And so, too, did the ways he did violence to the natural world.

Prophetic Warnings

There were rumblings of the troubles that were coming. Prophets arose in America. If they did not always see the harm that was being visited upon nature, they recognized the worth of the blessings she conferred upon us.

One great seer was Ralph Waldo Emerson, the Concord minister. Emerson revered nature. "In the woods is perpetual youth," he said. "In the woods, we return to reason and faith. . . . There . . . the currents of the Universal Being circulate through me; I am part or parcel of God."

His friend the writer Henry David Thoreau raised his voice against the desecration of the woodland and the injury done to its wildlife by lumbermen. "Every creature," declared Thoreau, the sage of Walden, "is better alive than dead, men and moose, and pine trees, and he who understands it aright will rather preserve its life than destroy it."

John Muir, the great naturalist, walked on foot across much of the country. Only one who knew nature from long, close fellowship, as he did, could appreciate her true value. Loggers were cutting down the age-old redwoods of California — the tallest of living things — and Muir worked tirelessly to stop them. The fight was exhausting, but the reward was great. Legislators enlarged the Yosemite reservation and set aside millions of acres of wilderness under Federal protection.

We remember John Muir. In a time when honest, forthright speech was needed, he was not ashamed or afraid to speak up. He was attacked and reviled, but still he did not falter. He lashed out at those who wanted to take over the great parklands. "These temple destroyers, devotees of ravaging commercialism, seem to have a perfect contempt for Nature," he thundered, "and, instead of lifting their eyes to the God of the Mountains, lift them to the Almighty Dollar."

To John Muir we owe the preservation of much of our national heritage in the West. Muir Woods National Monument in California, with its great redwoods, is worthily named in his honor.

Presidents Who Saved the Land

John Muir was a friend and camping companion of Theodore Roosevelt. Under Muir's influence Roosevelt became our great conservationist President. He saved vast domains of wilderness from the "land thieves," as he called them. To him we owe five of our national parks.

In a message to Congress, he said:

"To waste, to destroy, our natural resources, to skin and exhaust the land instead of using it so as to increase its usefulness, will result in undermining in the days of our children the very prosperity which we ought by right to hand down to them amplified and developed."

In the thirties, the era of the "dust bowl," Franklin Delano Roosevelt carried reforestation and land renewal programs forward on a large scale. He saved millions and millions of acres of eroded, wasted land. He endeavored to put the physical development of our country on a planned basis.

After Roosevelt came other great lovers and protectors of the land. One was John F. Kennedy. To President Kennedy conservation was "the highest form of national thrift — the prevention of waste and despoilment while preserving, improving and renewing the quality and usefulness of all our national resources." And with his deeds he upheld his words.

It is in our own time that concern over the despoilment of our resources and the pollution of the natural environment has come to a head. Each year the problem has grown more pressing. In the words of President Richard M. Nixon, "The nineteen-seventies absolutely must be the years when America pays its debt to the past by reclaiming the purity of its air, its waters and our living environment. It is literally now or never."

45

Tools of Our Salvation

Can we — will we — move fast enough to reclaim the earth and turn it into the Eden it can become?

The tools of our salvation are in our hands, waiting to be used.

We can restrict the size of our families so the population remains stable and does not overwhelm the land and exhaust it.

Already we have machinery that can swallow up the solid waste that disfigures the landscape — machinery that can separate metals and other substances and save them to be used again.

We have built pilot plants that can take garbage and other refuse and burn them without pollution to produce electric power.

Our engineers have invented countless other ways to control pollution of the air, land and water.

The cost of installing and using the new machines and methods will be heavy. We will all have to pay more to live in a safer, pollution-free world. But if we use our knowledge and power wisely, we should be able to save our endangered planet and ourselves.

If we say yes to life — if we are willing to pay the price — we may still be able to bring Eden back to earth.

Charles Kingsley wrote:

"Oh, the splendor of the universe! For many of us autumntime is the most glorious of all the year.

"God his dipped His paint brush in His palette of colors and splashed the hills and woods and fields with robes of saffron and crimson and gold and yellow and brown and scarlet.

"The maples and chestnuts and oaks vie with one another in autumnal beauty. The sumac dazzles the eye with brilliant scarlet. The sunsets are too gorgeous for human description.

"In this amazing garden of beauty our lips involuntarily sing forth the praises of the psalmist: 'Bless Jehovah, O my soul; and all this is within me, bless his holy name.' "

Chapter 9
THE GARDEN OF EDEN

And God blessed the seventh day, and sanctified it: because that in it he had rested from all his work which God created and made . . .

And the Lord God planted a garden eastward in Eden; and there he put the man whom he had formed.

Genesis 2:3, 8

A new Eden is within our reach. We can use science and technology not to destroy this planet but to rebuild it. We can make earth like the blessed garden that God planted for us, His children, long ago. But the undertaking will be arduous, and everyone, young and old, must do his part. Everyone must work to restore the environment and protect it, not just today and tomorrow . . . not just this year and next . . . but every day and every year, until the end of time.

"The task of cleaning up our environment," President Richard M. Nixon told us a few years ago, "calls for a total mobilization by all of us . . . it requires the help of every citizen. It cannot be a matter of simply sitting back and blaming someone else. Neither is it one to be left to a few hundred leaders . . . This task is ours together. It summons our energy, our ingenuity, and our conscience in a cause as fundamental as life itself."

Government Must Lead

Government must lead the way — and it is leading, through the Environmental Protection Agency. The National Environmental Policy Act, signed into law by the President on January 1, 1970, established a national program to "maintain conditions under which man and nature can exist in productive harmony, and fulfill the social, economic, and other requirements of present and future generations of Americans." The agency is mounting an attack on the problems of air and water pollution, solid-waste management, radiation, noise, and pesticides.

But the Federal Government can only regulate under Federal law, on matters of national concern. And it moves very slowly and is subject to pressures from powerful groups. For direct local help and control we must look to our states and our cities.

More and more states and cities are adopting environmental policies and programs. More and more are passing strong laws or firmly enforcing laws that have been long on the books. Regional agencies are also being formed by states that share a common environmental problem. For example, the states that surround the Great Lakes share the responsibility for keeping the lakes clean, and so does Canada. All must work together in the common cause.

How Industry Can Help

Many industries are cooperating in the national effort to curb pollution. But not all. All should — and must.

Plants must install devices on their chimneys to control smoke emissions, harmful gases, and other pollutants. Some emissions can be reused — and they should be. It is possible to collect oils, ammonia, and other emitted substances and use them in the manufacture of chemicals — instead of discharging them into the troubled air. Sulfur dioxide, a dangerous waste produced when coal and oil are burned, can be trapped and made into sulfuric acid, which has wide industrial usage.

Paper, bottles, and cans can be recycled and given a new life. Materials that cannot be recycled can be burned to provide power.

Food processors and manufacturers should use no more preservatives than are absolutely necessary — and only those that have been tested adequately.

Farmers can choose pesticides that will exterminate only their insect targets. They can take many other steps to control injurious insects. They can delay their ploughing until the soil is full of insect larvae, and then destroy them with their ploughshares. They can rotate their crops so that insects that feed on just a single kind of plant will starve. They can introduce beneficial insects like the ladybird, which feed on harmful insects.

Join in the Battle

In the battle to save the environment, you, the private citizen, have a giant part to play. It is made up of many small tasks, but they are important ones.

If you are a homeowner, you should not burn leaves — make them into a compost heap if possible. Use insecticides sparingly. Plant trees and shrubs. Not only do they absorb poisonous carbon dioxide and purify the air; they also help to prevent soil erosion. Don't leave litter in streets or parks.

If you drive a car, use it no more than you have to, and don't leave the engine running when you're parked. Car exhaust is a dangerous pollutant. Get an engine tuneup regularly. Noise is harmful, too: don't use your horn if you don't need to, and keep your muffler and tailpipe in good condition. Make sure that your car is equipped with the antipollution devices the law requires.

At home, be certain to turn off the lights, the television, the air conditioner, and other electrical equipment when you don't need them. They help to use up the earth's irreplaceable resources of coal and oil. The burning of these fuels also contributes to pollution. Protect your pocketbook while you protect the environment.

Above all, let your voice be heard in the halls of government. When matters of ecology are at issue, let your elected representatives know your opinions. Support those that support the movement to protect the environment.

Be mindful, also, that many organizations are fighting in defense of the environment. The Audubon Society, the Wildlife Federation, the National Resources Defense Council are just a few of them. You can find out about these and other organizations from your local nature museum or library. Enroll in one of these groups and help it fight the good fight.

Join in the battle to save your world — to bring Eden back to earth — or you may wake up suddenly and find that this entire country is paved with concrete from sea to shining sea!

As the philosopher, Jose Ortega y Gasset, wrote: "I am myself and what is around me, and if I do not save it, it shall not save me."

Chapter 10
MUST WE BE DRIVEN OUT?

Therefore the Lord God sent him forth from the garden of Eden, to till the ground from whence he was taken.

So he drove out the man; and he placed at the east of the garden of Eden Cherubims, and a flaming sword which turned every way, to keep the way of the tree of life.

Genesis 3:23, 24

In Bible times, Adam and Eve disobeyed the Lord's command and He drove them out of the Garden of Eden. In our own day, we have been disobedient to the counsel of wisdom that we cherish the earth and we have disregarded laws of nature. If we do not mend our ways quickly and completely, we may find ourselves on a dying planet — a planet that can no longer support our life.

Lately, we have begun to restore the damage we have done to our environment. But we move at a snail's pace. And we falter. Often we seem to take one step forward — and two steps back.

Although the United States, Canada, and some other countries are taking measures to combat pollution, many other countries do nothing at all. The state of the land, the seas, and the air should be the concern of everyone. Pesticides and radioactive fallout do not stop at national boundaries; they waft their way around and around the globe. The United Nations could promote the ecological welfare of the entire world, but so far has done little about it.

Many of the nations, especially the emerging ones, are complacent about the threat to the environment. The haze of pollution that overhangs their cities to them is a mark of achievement. To them, pollution means that they are catching up with the advanced industrial powers! But smog is not a sign of success.

In the black cloud of pollution ride the Four Horsemen of the Apocalypse.

Journey to Other Planets

In the United States and other developed countries the population has ceased to increase as sharply as it used to. In the newer, underdeveloped countries, however, the birth rate continues to boom. Four out of ten people in the countries of Asia, Africa, and Latin America are under fifteen years of age.

In the next ten years these multitudes of young people will marry and have children — more children than the world has ever seen . . . or ever should. The drain on the earth's resources, the worldwide pollution, the hunger, and suffering will be without precedent.

Some persons say that we do not really have to worry as the earth's peoples double in number — and double again. Technological progress, they say, has solved our problems in the past; it will solve them again. We have already made a start in space travel. If we put our best minds to work, we can design great space transports, and these can lift our excess population to another planet. We can continue to live the free and easy life here, polluting and wasting. And, on that other planet, the rest of mankind can live the same way.

Our present population on earth is 3.5 billion. In thirty-five years or so it will double. Suppose that, over the next thirty-five years, we send the increase in our population to Mercury or Mars. At the end of the period, on earth we would have the same population we do at present. And the population of Mercury or Mars would match ours. Seven billion souls, all told.

But what of the thirty-five years that follow?

In that period — or less — the population of the earth and that other planet would double. Seven billion people would become fourteen billion. They would have to be transported to other planets, and others. In a few generations the entire solar system would become as crowded as the earth is now.

Where would we turn next — to Andromeda and other galaxies, millions and billions of light years away?

It is an awesome fantasy. But it is no more than a fantasy.

Earth Is Our Space Ark

It is idle to think of sending our excess population to other planets in space arks. Earth itself is our space ark. To keep its life-support systems intact, we must limit our numbers. We must cooperate again with nature — give her fruitful cycles time to renew themselves. If we do, our ship can go on and on, carrying us in safety and comfort as it has done through ages past.

It is no easy job that lies before us.

We must change habits that have gone unquestioned for generations.

We must stop throwing things away. We must repair them, recycle them, use them again.

We must stop discharging our wastes into the air and water. We must find harmless, useful ways to dispose of them.

Instead of wasting our resources, we must handle them with care, with thrift. We must make them last.

Instead of killing animals, we must protect them.

When we cut down a tree, we must plant two in its place.

Sterling North wrote: "We are but the ephemera of the moment, the brief custodians of redwods, which were ancient when Christ was born, and of the birds of the air and animals of the forest which have been evolving for countless millenniums. We do not own the land we abuse, or the lakes and streams we pollute or the raccoons and the otters which we persecute. Those who play God in destroying any form of life are tampering with a master plan too intricate for any of us to understand."

God's Purpose

God has made His purpose manifest to us; the renewal of life and the earth. We see it in the fertile egg, the swelling seed, the green leaf, the opening blossom and the changing seasons.

God's purpose — and nature's — is not to poison life or destroy it, but to perpetuate it.

His purpose is not to weaken life — but to strengthen it.

His purpose is not to lay waste the earth — but to make it fruitful, to deck it with garlands.

He offers us a simple choice. We can walk in His way — nature's way, and live — or continue on the road to self-destruction.

If we have the wish — if we have the will — we can rebuild the kind of world God made for us. We can have again a beautiful world, not only for ourselves but for our children and our grandchildren — and for their children.

We do not need to journey far in search of Eden.

We need only to cultivate our own garden, Earth.

By following God's plan, each of us can find Eden — right here on earth.

Acknowledgments

The editor and the publisher have made every effort to trace the ownership of all copyrighted material and to secure permission from copyright holders of such material. In the event of any question arising as to the use of any material the publisher and editor, while expressing regret for inadvertent error, will be pleased to make the necessary corrections in future printings. Thanks are due to the following publishers for permission to use the material indicated.

E. P. DUTTON & CO., INC., for selection from *Raccoons Are the Brightest People* by Sterling North, copyright 1966 by Sterling North.

HOLT, RINEHART AND WINSTON, INC. for selection from "The Sound of Trees" from *The Poetry of Robert Frost* edited by Edward Connery Latham. Copyright 1916, © 1969 by Holt, Rinehart and Winston, Inc. Copyright 1944 by Robert Frost.

FREDERICK WARNE & CO., INC. for selection from *The Journal of Beatrix Potter from 1881 to 1897*. Copyright © 1966 by Frederick Warne & Company, Ltd.